HANDMADE
Gift Cards

HANDMADE
Gift Cards

Over 50 original designs for all occasions

Cheryl Owen

David & Charles

A DAVID & CHARLES BOOK

First published in the UK in hardback 2001
Reprinted 2002
First published in the UK in paperback 2002

Distributed in paperback in North America
by F&W Publications Inc.
4700 E. Galbraith Rd.
Cincinnati, OH 45236
1-800-289-0963

ISBN 0 7153 1177 8 (hardback)
ISBN 0 7153 1268 5 (paperback)

Commissioning editor Lindsay Porter
Art editor Ali Myer
Desk editor Jennifer Proverbs
Text editor Lin Clements
Photography Amanda Heywood
Designer Caroline Reeves

Printed in Hong Kong by Dai Nippon
for David & Charles
Brunel House   Newton Abbot   Devon

*The author has made every effort to ensure that all the instructions in this
book are accurate and safe, and therefore cannot accept liability for any
resulting injury, damage or loss to persons or property, however it may arise.*

Contents

Introduction

Gift cards are exchanged throughout the year, either to mark special occasions or simply to keep in touch with loved ones, and giving a hand-crafted card shows the recipient that you care enough to do more than just purchase an unoriginal, ready-made version. Indeed, many of us who do not usually involve ourselves with craft activities like to make gift cards, as beautiful results can be achieved so quickly and inexpensively and no special equipment is needed.

This book presents lots of innovative ideas for both the beginner and the accomplished card maker. There is a paper crafts chapter on some of the many wonderful ways paper can be transformed and another chapter devoted to using exciting mixed media materials. There are gift-card projects to mark all red-letter days, and they are all accompanied by concise step-by-step instructions with inspiring photographs and further ideas using the techniques involved. Apart from the wealth of cards created using all sorts of different materials, there are also projects in the book suggesting ways to display cherished gift cards and to keep them safe.

You may be surprised to find how quickly some gift cards can be made if, for example, you want to produce multiples for Christmas, party invitations, a change of address or a birth announcement. Alternatively, you could lavish time and care creating a one-off card to commemorate a milestone event which will be much treasured by the recipient.

Keep an eye out for interesting papers and components that you can incorporate into your cards. Only small quantities of materials are needed and you will soon be seeing everyday items in a new light. Collect twigs and fallen leaves, pretty labels and scraps of fabric – they will all make great finishing touches to your creations. Read through the instructions before you embark on a project, then have fun experimenting with the various techniques outlined in the book and creating your own designs.

All sorts of unexpected materials can be incorporated into your creations.

7

Decorative Papers

The wonderful array of paper and card that is widely available nowadays is very enticing. Art shops and specialist paper shops have papers from all over the world. Prices vary and a sheet of handmade textured paper, although expensive, will go a long way and make a selection of very special cards. There are superb tactile papers available embedded with various materials such as flower petals, grasses and fragments of fabric and yarn. If you cannot find the exact paper you have in mind for a project, you may be tempted to create your own. You may also like to experiment with marbled papers – they are exciting to create yourself but can also be bought by the sheet.

High-class stationery shops sell single sheets of writing paper. They are always good quality and mean you can buy the exact quantity needed rather than a whole pad or box of papers. As they are of standard sizes, you will be able to buy matching envelopes.

Mass-produced card and paper come in masses of colours, thicknesses and finishes. Some have a special coating on one side giving pearlized, metallic and futuristic holographic effects. Wood-effect papers and miniature wallpaper and tile designs intended for dolls' houses are unusual papers to use for making cards. Wood veneer paper is a wafer-thin layer of wood on a paper backing: it can be expensive to buy but smells delightful. Crêpe paper, origami papers and gummed paper squares may at first remind you of the humble creations you once proudly brought home from primary school. However, they also have interesting 'grown-up' uses and are very economical to buy.

You can also recycle card and paper you have already. Cut out motifs from gift-wrap or left-over wallpaper to stick to a card for a quick and easy creation. Brown parcel paper and corrugated card can be used for a natural effect or spray painted in vibrant colours. Fine tissue papers can be spray glued to firmer papers to make them easier to handle. Metal foil sweet papers and even paper doilies can be used as decorations and ready-made stickers will provide an instant burst of colour. Remember that you only need small scraps of pretty papers to give your cards a stunning finishing touch.

Tactile, textured papers, such as those opposite, give a three-dimensional feel to gift cards.

9

Embellishments

There is an endless choice of materials that can be used to embellish gift cards. Even the tiniest, understated decorations can make your creations look extra special.

You probably have many items around your home that can be incorporated into your card making – wire, coloured stickers, patterned paper bags, waxed paper drink cartons and printed metal tins are all suitable. Use your imagination to think up new ways of using everyday items to enhance your gift cards.

Save charms and beads from broken jewellery to add a glamorous three-dimensional element to your designs. Cabochon jewellery stones, for example, add a note of sophistication with their smooth, polished surface. Sequins are very inexpensive to buy and come in many shapes and colours. Sequin dust, which is available from specialist bead shops, is made up of the tiny holes punched from sew-on sequins. The particles are larger than glitter but can be used in a similar way. Gold, aluminium and copper leaf is the ultimate indulgence, and is relatively expensive, but a little goes a long way. Use metal foil sweet papers too for cheery, shining effects.

Keep off-cuts of ribbon, lace, braid, strings of fine beads and embroidery threads. These can be put to good use to create delicate, feminine cards. Buttons are very versatile, too. Look also to nature to provide small objects that will evoke seaside holidays and country walks. Collect little shells, grasses and feathers and press flowers from the garden. Fragrant items like cinnamon sticks and lavender seeds have a lasting quality and will become treasured, scented keepsakes when applied to cards.

You will also need to consider the fragility of the embellishments if the cards are to be sent through the post – a padded or card envelope will offer some protection for delicate materials. Test that the adhesive used is strong enough to hold the embellishments – an envelope containing a blank card and a few loose items is probably not the surprise you intended for the recipient!

Save off-cuts of ribbon, trimmings and braid, spare buttons and sequins to use as decorations.

11

Techniques

The basic techniques of card making are very straightforward and are described in this chapter to provide a quick reference. All the projects are clearly explained with step-by-step, illustrated instructions, plus a list of the specific tools and materials you will need.

You will find it useful to have some basic tools and materials to hand. These include drawing pens and pencils, coloured pencils and felt-tipped pens, sharp scissors (for paper and fabric), craft knife, metal ruler, cutting board, scrap paper, tracing paper, masking tape, double-sided adhesive tape, spray adhesive, all-purpose adhesives (such as glue sticks, PVA, Bostik and UHU), sewing and embroidery needles and an iron.

Using Templates

The twenty main projects are accompanied by templates, to make drawing easier for you.

1 If you intend to use a template often, maybe to make a series of cards, glue it to thin card with spray adhesive before you cut it out; this will make it more durable.

2 You may prefer to draw directly on to the material you wish to use. Always use a ruler and set square so that straight lines and right angles are accurate, giving neat results. A sharp HB or propelling pencil is best for drawing. Throughout each project, refer to either metric *or* imperial measurements, but not both.

3 To transfer a traced design on to paper or card, redraw it on the wrong side of the tracing with a pencil. Tape the tracing face up on paper or card and redraw it to transfer the design.

Cutting

Straight edges are best cut with a craft knife or scalpel rather than a pair of scissors.

1 Always use a craft knife or scalpel resting on a cutting mat and cut straight lines against a metal ruler. When cutting card, do not press too hard or attempt to cut right through at the first approach, but gradually cut deeper and deeper.

2 Change the blades regularly as a blunt blade will tear the paper surface. Take great care when handling the blades.

Scoring and Folding

Scoring card will make it easier to fold and give a neat finish.

I A bone folder is a traditional bookbinding tool and, although not essential, it is very useful for scoring and folding if you intend to make a lot of gift cards. Score card with the pointed end of a bone folder against a ruler. Keep the movement smooth and even as you go. If you do not have a bone folder, score lightly with a craft knife, taking great care *not* to cut right through the card, but to break the top surface only.

2 To fold card or paper, press the bone folder flat on the card and run it along the fold. Again, keep the movement smooth and even as you go. Alternatively, do this with your thumb.

Using Adhesives

The cards in this book mainly use all-purpose household glues, PVA and spray adhesive.

I All-purpose household glues such as glue sticks, UHU and Bostik are very versatile and can be used to glue a range of cards and papers and other lightweight fabrics and items. PVA (polyvinyl acetate) is another general-purpose adhesive, useful for gluing on items such as pressed flowers, sequins and shredded tissue.

2 Always test an adhesive first on a scrap of material to make sure it is the right glue for the job and actually sticks. Ensure it does not seep to the right side on fabrics, ribbons or fine papers.

3 Spray adhesives glue paper and card together smoothly and are good for sticking large surface areas together. Always spray the adhesive in a well-ventilated room and protect the surrounding area with newspaper.

4 Strengthen thin paper by gluing the paper to thin card with spray adhesive. Roughly cut the paper and card larger than the gift card will be. Spray the wrong side of the paper with spray adhesive and stick it to the card, then cut out the greetings card. Use contrasting colours for a dramatic effect.

Using Bondaweb

Bondaweb (Wonder-Under) is a product by Vilene. It sticks fabric to fabric or card, and helps prevent fabric from fraying when handled.

Draw a mirror image of your design on the paper-backing of the Bondaweb. Roughly cut out the shape and iron it on to the wrong side of the fabric. Cut out the design. Peel off the backing and position it right side up on the fabric or card. Iron the motif to fuse it in place.

Creating Deckle Edges

A natural-looking torn edge is easy to achieve and gives a delicate hand-crafted touch to cards.

1 Place a ruler on the paper where you wish to tear it. Paint a line against the ruler with water to soften the card or paper. If the card is very thick, you may need to do this on the reverse of the card too.

2 Hold the ruler firmly on the paper and tear the paper against it.

Making a Window Card

Ready-made window card blanks are widely available in a huge range of styles. However, it is very easy to make your own.

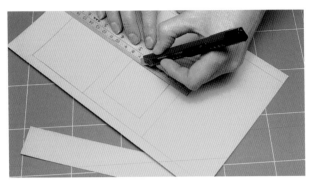

1 To make a template, draw the dimensions of the front of the card and its window on scrap paper. Draw the back adjoining the left-hand side of the front the same size and the facing adjoining the right-hand side 5mm (¼in) narrower. Use the template to cut out the card from thin card or thick paper. Thick card is unsuitable as it will be too bulky when folded – a suitable weight of paper would be 190gsm.

2 Score the card along the lines with a bone folder or craft knife. Fold the facing, along the scored lines, inside the card. Open out the card again. Glue the motif to the facing so it shows through the window. If the motif is transparent or does not fill the window, glue a piece of white paper to the facing first as a background. Glue the facing to the underside of the front with double-sided adhesive tape.

Making an Insert

An insert within a card provides an added touch of style. It is useful if the interior of the card is dark in colour, as a pale insert gives an interesting contrast and can be written on in any colour.

1 Fold a sheet of paper in half for the insert. Cut it 5mm (¼in) smaller than the card front.

2 Run a line of paper glue (such as a glue stick) close to the fold and stick it inside the back of the gift card, matching the folds.

Making Holes

Holes will need to be made in the cards and envelopes for many reasons. Use a thick needle to make small holes. Use a bradawl to enlarge the holes if necessary. A hole punch is useful for larger holes, maybe to thread cord, ribbon or leather thongs through.

Making Stickers

Small, intricately cut elements of a design are often too fiddly to be stuck in place with glue, so double-sided adhesive tape is a very practical alternative. The adhesive tape has a paper backing that can be peeled off when you are ready to use each individual sticker, allowing you to make batches if making a series of cards.

1 Stick double-sided tape to the wrong side of the paper. Draw the motifs on the backing tape and then cut them out.

2 Peel off the backing tapes and stick the motifs in place. (Use the tip of a craft knife to lift the edge of the backing tape if necessary.)

Attaching Studs

Metal studs can be used for decoration and to fix layers of paper, card and even plastic together. They are widely available, and come in lots of shapes and sizes.

1 Push the prongs of the studs through the card – you may need to pierce holes first with a needle.

2 Fold the prongs over the back of the card with your fingers or with the blade of a pair of scissors, making sure they lie flat against the card.

Making a Tassel

A flamboyant tassel gives an excellent finishing touch to a gift card or envelope. Any sort of yarn is suitable, from fine embroidery thread to chunky knitting wool (yarn).

1 Cut a rectangle of card 10 x 5cm (4 x 2in) and fold in half. Wind yarn around the folded edge of the card numerous times, depending on the thickness of the tassel needed.

2 Fold a short length of yarn in half and thread the ends through the eye of a tapestry needle. Thread the needle behind the strands close to the fold, then insert the needle through the loop of the yarn and pull tightly.

3 Slip the point of a pair of sharp scissors between the two layers of card and cut through the loops. Discard the card.

4 Thread a single length of yarn on to the needle. Bind the yarn tightly around the head of the tassel, gathering it together tightly. To secure, insert the needle into the bulk of the tassel to loose the end of the yarn within the tassel. Cut the ends of the fringe level.

Making a Basic Envelope

Your gift cards may well fit standard-size envelopes. If not, it is easy to make them yourself, or you may wish to make your own so that it coordinates with the card.

1 Make a template first by measuring the card front and drawing it on scrap paper adding 3mm (⅛in) to each edge. Draw the flap at the upper edge half the depth of the front. Draw the back at the lower edge, taking 2cm (¾in) off the depth. Draw a tab at each side of the front 2.5cm (1in) wide. Draw a curve at each corner.

2 Now cut out this envelope shape to use as a template. Draw around the template on paper or thin card. Fold along the lines, folding the tabs under the back.

3 Open out the back again. Apply 1.2cm (½in) wide double-sided adhesive tape along the side edges of the back on the wrong side. Peel off the backing tapes and stick over the tabs. Tuck the flap inside the envelope or seal it with double-sided tape.

Making a Lined Envelope

A contrast-coloured lining is a pleasant surprise when the recipient opens an envelope. Use a thin paper for the lining so the envelope is not too bulky.

1 Cut out the basic envelope as described opposite. Cut the front and flap from the lining paper, trimming 3mm (⅛in) from the outer edges. Glue the lining to the wrong side of the envelope 3mm (⅛in) inside the edges with spray adhesive.

2 Continue making up the envelope as before, but tuck the flap into the envelope rather than gluing it.

Making a Padded Envelope

Delicate greetings cards can be presented in padded envelopes for protection.

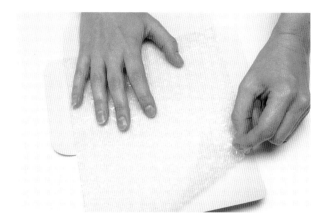

I Measure the card front and draw it on scrap paper adding 1cm (⅜in) to each edge. Draw up the envelope referring to the basic envelope instructions on page 17, then cut out the envelope. Cut the front and back from bubble wrap or thin foam. Glue these pieces to the wrong side of the envelope with spray adhesive, with the smooth side of the bubble wrap uppermost.

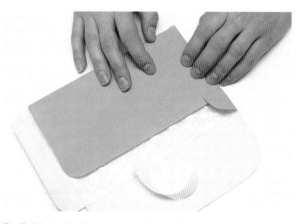

2 Fold the back over the front. Glue the tabs over the back with 1.2cm (½in) wide double-sided tape, pressing firmly to ensure the package is secure. Fold the flap over the back to finish.

Making a Classic Wallet Envelope

This simple envelope has no flap and so lends itself to lots of interesting fastening features.

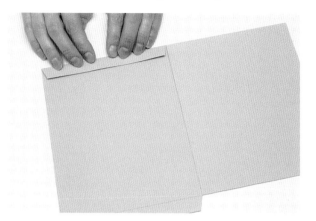

I To make a template, measure the card front and draw it on scrap paper, adding 2cm (¾in) to the upper edge and 3mm (⅛in) to the other edges. Draw the back at the lower edge the same size as the front. Draw a tab at each side of the front 1.5cm (⅝in) wide. Draw a slanted edge at the end of each tab. Cut out this shape to use as a template. Cut out the envelope from paper or thin card, then fold the envelope along the lines, folding the tabs under the back.

2 Glue the back over the tabs with double-sided adhesive tape. The envelope can be fastened by fixing eyelets through the upper edges, or by punching holes and tying with ribbon, cord or thonging.

Making a Quick Wallet Envelope

This instant wallet can be made from a single sheet of paper.

I Simply fold a rectangle of paper or card in half and stick the edges together with double-sided tape or paper glue. Here, the wallet has been cut from wallpaper with its motif centred on the front.

2 Make a quick envelope with a flap by folding a rectangle of paper or card into three. Stick the edges together with double-sided adhesive tape or paper glue.

Making a Box Envelope

A three-dimensional card looks wonderful if presented in a custom-made box. For added protection, glue a piece of bubble wrap or fine foam in the lid and wrap the card in tissue paper or fill the box with shredded tissue.

I To make a template, measure the card front and draw it on scrap paper, adding 3mm ($^1/_8$ in) to each edge. Lay the gift card flat and measure its depth. Draw a side to the box along each edge that is the depth of the card plus 3mm ($^1/_8$ in). Add a 1.5cm ($^5/_8$ in) wide tab to both ends of two opposite box sides, draw a slanted end to each tab.

2 Cut out the template and use it to cut a box from card. Score along the lines with a bone folder or craft knife and fold the sides upwards. Glue the tabs under the end of the opposite box sides with double-sided adhesive tape. Make a lid in the same way as for the box but adding 2mm ($^1/_{16}$ in) to each edge of the base.

Paper Crafts

Paper is, of course, the obvious and most important material for card making and this chapter explores some of the many exciting ways of working with paper and transforming its appearance. Using the correct weight of paper and card is very important and, generally, 190–280gsm are good weights to use. Use a heavyweight card if weighty decorations are to be stuck to it.

If cards are to be painted, test the paint on a scrap of the intended paper to make sure that it does not wrinkle or warp the surface. There are lots of easy-to-use craft paints available. Acrylic paints in particular are very versatile: there are many colours that can be mixed together to create other shades; the paints are easy to apply and they dry quickly. Watercolour paints also blend together well. They are ideally used on watercolour paper but can be painted on to other surfaces too. Metallic and pearlized paints give lovely, sophisticated effects and glitter paint adds a touch of sparkle if you want to add a festive, party mood to a card.

Sponging paint on to paper is a fast and simple way to transform its appearance. Lightly dab at the paint with a moistened natural sponge then dab it on to the paper either at random all over the surface or in small areas.

Relief paint pens are tubes of paint that can be drawn on the card and will dry proud of the surface; pearlized and glitter paint pens also produce great effects. Alternatively, draw with coloured felt-tipped pens for quick results.

As well as painting and drawing on paper, there are many other exciting ways to change its appearance. The following ideas show, among other techniques, how to pin prick designs or cut away intricate shapes to allow a different coloured paper to show through. Experiment with as many of the different techniques as you can – your rough experiments can even be made into a collage-style gift card. Most of the projects that follow have templates provided, and there are instructions in Techniques page 12 for using templates.

All kinds of paper can be painted, pin-pricked and cut, to create unusual and original designs.

21

Concertina Notecards

A concertina notecard opens out to allow lots of space for writing a letter or including photographs or maybe holiday souvenirs.

This vibrant card has a window cut in the front to reveal a flower picture cut from coloured papers. Alternatively, you could glue a motif cut from gift-wrap or a photograph in the window. Fasten the card with coloured elastic for the recipient to open.

You Will Need

Thick turquoise paper
Craft knife, metal ruler and cutting mat
Bone folder (optional)
Paper – pink, purple, yellow and
    jade green
Double-sided tape 1.2cm (½in) and
    2.5cm (1in) wide

Pair of fancy-edged scissors
Hole punch
Spray adhesive
40cm (½yd) pink elastic
Two purple heart-shaped beads

1 Cut the thick turquoise paper 40 x 17cm (16 x 6¾in) with a craft knife, resting on a cutting mat. Score across the length at 10cm (4in) intervals with a bone folder or craft knife. Fold the scored lines in alternate directions to create a concertina. Open out flat, then mark and cut out the window according to the measurements given in the diagram.

2 Apply a length of 1.2cm (½in) wide double-sided adhesive tape to the wrong side of a piece of pink paper along the width. Draw a 6mm (¼in) wide strip on the backing tape. Cut one edge with a craft knife and the other with fancy-edged scissors. Cut into four 5cm (2in) lengths and stick along each edge of the right side of the window.

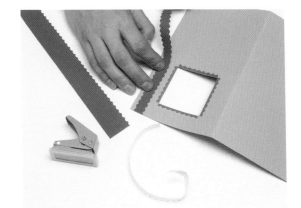

Paisley Concertina Card
A bold paisley motif decorates this circular card. Apply double-sided adhesive tape to the papers the decorations will be cut from. This is easier and cleaner than using glue.

Fern Concertina Card
Fancy-edged scissors produce a delicate border to the triangular motif. Choose contrasting coloured papers to really emphasize the design.

3 Apply 1.2cm (¹/₂ in) wide double-sided tape to the wrong side of a piece of purple paper. Cut a 1.2cm (¹/₂ in) wide strip with fancy-edged scissors. Peel off the backing tape and stick along the opening edge on the front of the card, cutting off the excess strip. Punch a hole in the centre of the strip with a hole punch.

4 Using the flower template given here, cut the flower and stem from scrap paper. Apply a piece of 2.5cm (1in) wide double-sided tape to the back of the yellow and jade green paper. Trace the flower on to the tape of the yellow paper, and the stem on to the paper tape of the jade green paper, then cut out.

5 Cut a 7cm (2¾in) square of purple paper with fancy-edged scissors. Peel the backing tapes off the flowers and stem and stick them to the purple square. Glue the picture inside the card with spray adhesive. Write your message in the card.

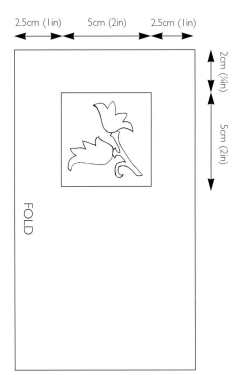

6 To fasten, close the card and thread pink elastic through the punched hole, then thread a bead on each end and knot the elastic under the beads. Wrap the elastic around the card and tie the ends together on the front.

Enlarge template by 200%

25

Pop Ups

A pop-up card has a surprise inside, for when the flap on the card front is opened it reveals a hidden motif suspended inside. Once you have mastered the basic technique, you will be able to design your own versions of this ingenious card.

A silver moon hides behind a smiling sun face on this celestial gift card. The golden rays of the sun are sponged with gold paint and the face is drawn with a gold relief paint pen.

YOU WILL NEED

Cream card
Craft knife, metal ruler and cutting mat
Gold craft paint
Ceramic tile
Flat paintbrush

Natural sponge
Gold relief paint pen
All-purpose household glue
Bone folder (optional)
Silver card

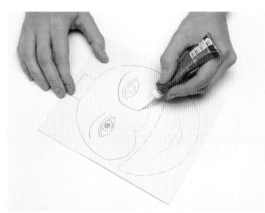

1 Using the sun template provided and the cream card, cut out the sun following the wavy-edged rays, using a craft knife and cutting mat. (The straight-edged rays shape is for the star variation card on page 29.) Place the sun on a sheet of scrap paper. With a flat paintbrush, put some gold paint on to a ceramic tile. Dab at the paint with a moistened natural sponge and then dab it on to the rays of the sun.

2 In pencil, draw the lower face of the sun on cream card, following the curved, dotted lines on the template, and drawing the lips with a gold relief pen. Draw the upper face of the sun on cream card, drawing the nose, eyes and cheeks in gold relief pen. Once dry, cut the lower and upper face pieces out.

3 Apply a 5mm (¼in) wide band of all-purpose glue to the outer curve on the wrong side of the lower face, then stick this to the sun.

4 Score along the broken tab line on the upper face and bend the tab to the underside of the upper face. Glue the tab to the top of the sun, below the top sun ray.

5 Using the moon template provided, cut out a moon from silver card and cut out the eye. Score along the broken tab line. Open the upper face of the sun and lightly mark the moon tab position on the underside of the upper face, then glue the moon tab in place. Leave the glue to dry then close the upper face, slipping the lower edge of the moon inside the lower face.

6 Using the stand template provided, cut a stand from cream card. Score along the broken tab line and bend the tab backwards. Position the lower edge of the stand and the lower points of the sun rays level by resting them against a ruler, then glue the tab to the back of the sun.

Glittering Star Card

Using the sun template, make a star of turquoise card, cutting a circle for the card front and a half circle using the lower face template, but cutting the rays along the straight dotted lines. Apply gold glitter paint to the circle and the rays. Draw sparkly stars on the front with a silver relief paint pen. A Christmas angel or space rocket, cut out of white card and decorated with a gold relief paint pen, could be placed inside.

UPPER FACE TAB

UPPER FACE

POSITION OF MOON TAB

LOWER FACE

TAB

STAND

TAB

MOON

Enlarge templates by 200%

Transparent Paper

Initially we may not think of using delicate transparent papers for card making, but there are lovely coloured transparent papers in various thicknesses available from art and specialist paper shops. Fixing layers of different coloured transparent papers together creates varying hues and delicate, filmy effects.

Floral motifs lend themselves particularly well to the delicate quality of transparent papers. Here, an elegant allium is drawn with felt-tipped pens on a sheer paper. The drawing is fixed to the card front with a pair of metal eyelets.

YOU WILL NEED

Tracing paper
Craft knife, metal ruler and cutting mat
Transparent pink paper
Masking tape
Fine felt-tipped pens – pink and green
White-speckled transparent paper
White card

Spray adhesive
Bone folder (optional)
Transparent blue paper
Bright pink tissue paper
Bradawl
Two small chrome eyelets
Eyelet fixing tool

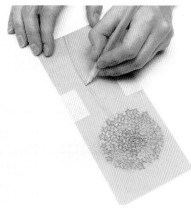

1 Trace the allium template. Cut a 21 x 8.5cm (8¼ x 3⅜in) rectangle of transparent pink paper. Stick the pink paper on the tracing with masking tape. Draw five-sided stars up to the outer circle with a fine pink felt-tipped pen. Dot the centre of each star.

2 Trace the stem of the allium with a green felt-tipped pen, then remove the tracing.

3 Stick white-speckled transparent paper to white card with spray adhesive. With a craft knife, metal ruler and a cutting mat, cut a rectangle 23 x 21cm (9 x 8¼in). Score across the centre, parallel with the long edges, using a bone folder or craft knife.

4 Fold the card in half. Cut the lower part (shown on the template) from transparent blue paper and stick this across the bottom of the card front with spray adhesive.

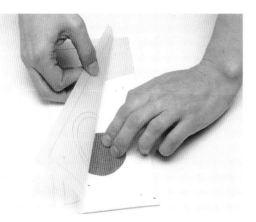

5 Use the allium template to cut the inner circle from bright pink tissue paper. Place the tracing on the front of the card and stick the circle to the card front with spray adhesive, using the tracing as a guide for positioning.

6 Mark the dots on the pink rectangle. Open the card out flat and position the picture centrally on the card front. Make a hole through the dots with a bradawl and then fix the picture to the card front with an eyelet through each hole. Refold the card in half.

Blue Flower Card
This flower was photocopied on to transparent blue paper from a copyright-free book. It is fixed with a stud to the card front with a larger rectangle of ribbed white transparent paper behind.

Yellow Flower Card
A floral motif has been photocopied from a copyright-free book on to yellow transparent paper, cut out and stuck to a square of pink transparent paper with spray glue. That is then glued to a rectangle of pale blue transparent paper and applied to the front of the card with chunky chrome studs.

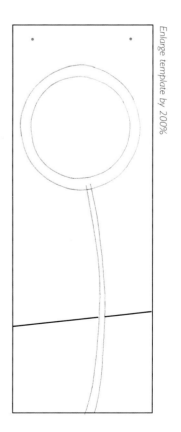

Enlarge template by 200%

33

Pin Pricking

It is surprising that a craft as simple as pricking designs on paper with a pin can yield such striking results. It is best to use a glass- or plastic-headed pin, as it will not hurt your fingers as an ordinary pin may do.

Here, a sea theme is emphasized with pricked wavy lines and pearl beads. Pearlized paper is used to make the scallop shell that is suspended within a framed window.

YOU WILL NEED

Pale blue-lilac mottled card
Craft knife, metal ruler and cutting mat
Bone folder (optional)
Kitchen paper towels
Glass- or plastic-headed
    dressmaking pin

One 8mm (¼in) pearl bead
Pale grey pearlized paper
Masking tape
White sewing thread
Small pearl beads

1 Cut a rectangle of pale blue-lilac card 30 x 15cm (12 x 6in) using a craft knife, metal ruler and cutting mat. Score across the centre with a bone folder or craft knife and fold in half. Open the card out flat again and use the template to cut out the window. Score along the broken lines and fold the scalloped edges outwards. Press the scallops out flat again.

2 Resting on about six sheets of kitchen towel, pin prick two rows of scallops around the edges of the window on the underside of the card, following the shape of the cut scalloped edge.

3 Turn the card to the right side and pin prick wavy lines on the card front: you could copy the wavy lines on the template or work freehand. Fold the scalloped edges of the window again and use an all-purpose glue to attach a large pearl bead to one scallop on the lower edge (see main photograph).

4 Using the shells template, trace and cut a scallop shell from scrap paper. Tape this template on to pale grey pearlized paper with masking tape and draw around the shell. Resting on kitchen towels, pin prick along the solid lines on the shell through the paper.

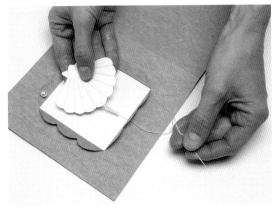

5 Remove the template and cut out the shell. Pierce a hole at the top for hanging. Thread a needle with a single length of white sewing thread and thread it through the hole.

6 Re-thread the needle with both ends of the thread so the thread is doubled. Thread on a few small pearl beads then insert the needle up through the centre of the fold on the upper edge of the window to suspend the shell in the middle of the window. Knot the thread in the fold and cut off the excess thread.

Enlarge templates by 200%

WINDOW

Seahorse Lantern

This flamboyant card would make a lovely home-warming gift. Holes are punched in the ends of the card and fastened together with ribbon to form a lantern. Pin-prick a seahorse design which will be highlighted by a candle. (Safety note: never leave a naked flame unattended.)

Sea and Shell card

A wavy edge is cut along the top of this card and torn slithers of white tissue paper stuck to the front with spray glue to suggest a foaming ocean. Pin-pricked shells cut from pearlized paper are applied with adhesive foam so that they stand proud of the card.

Paper Cuts

Intricate paper cuts are used in designs throughout the world. Although somewhat time consuming, the outcome is always stunning. For best results, cut carefully using a craft knife with a sharp blade, resting on a cutting mat. A small pair of sharp scissors can be used on thin papers if you prefer.

Chinese paper cuts are thought to bring good fortune. The charming Oriental willow pattern design is cut from watercolour paper and is then delicately painted. The design is applied to a card that stands like an easel to reflect the painterly quality of the design.

YOU WILL NEED

Tracing paper
Sheet of white watercolour paper
Masking tape
Craft knife, metal ruler and cutting mat
Watercolour paints – Chinese white,
    cobalt blue, turquoise and ultramarine

Ceramic tile or paint palette
Artist's paintbrush
Bone folder (optional)
White textured card
Spray adhesive

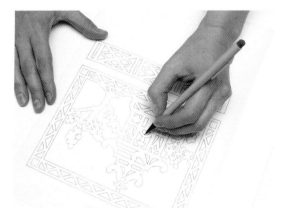

1 Using the picture and fence templates provided, trace them carefully on to tracing paper. Turn the tracing over and redraw on the underside with a pencil. Tape the tracings to a sheet of white watercolour paper and redraw to transfer the design.

2 Using a craft knife and resting on a cutting mat, carefully cut out the picture and the fence. Cut against a metal ruler for the straight edges.

3 Place the pieces on a sheet of scrap paper. Squeeze a little of each of the watercolour paints on to a ceramic tile or a palette. Thin the paints with water and paint the picture and fence, blending the colours together. Set aside to dry.

4 Cut textured white card 45.5 x 20cm (18 x 8in). Starting at one end, score widthways across the card, first 3.5cm (1½in) in, then 5cm (2in), and then 18.5cm (7¼in) from the end using a bone folder or a craft knife. Fold the card forward along the scored lines.

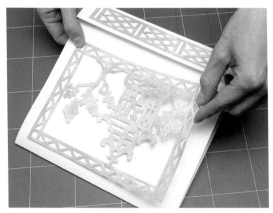

5 Open the card out flat again. With spray adhesive, glue the fence centrally to the narrow band of the card.

6 Tuck the other end of the card behind the fence band. Now apply spray adhesive to the underside of the picture and position it on the card front, above the fence. Open the card out flat to press the picture securely in place.

Oriental Flask Card

*Here, the delicate design from
an Oriental flask is cut from blue
gift-wrap and applied to the flask
cut from cream card.*

Fan Card

*This pretty card of white cutwork on
a deep blue background is finished
with an elegant tassel made from
stranded cotton (floss) embroidery
thread. The fan handle is cut from
light blue card and glued to the
folded edge of the card.*

Enlarge templates by 200%

41

Paper Collage

Mixing papers of different textures and thicknesses can create lavish effects. Paper is surprisingly resilient and can be gathered and pleated to imitate fabrics.

This theatrical card would be great to send to a fashion-loving friend. Exotic papers with metallic touches give a contemporary twist to a traditionally framed fashion plate. A flamboyant feather adds a tactile finishing touch to the glamorous shoe.

YOU WILL NEED

Craft knife, metal ruler and cutting mat
Cream card
Blue marbled paper
Spray adhesive
Paper – light blue, yellow ochre and gold
Fancy-edged scissors
Gold crêpe paper

Adhesive tape
All-purpose household glue
Pink marabou feather
Pink metallic card
Ribbed gold paper
Gold card
Bone folder (optional)

1 Cut a 13 x 9.5cm (5¼ x 3¾in) rectangle of cream card. Use the shoe template provided to cut a shoe upper from blue marbled paper (see page 12 for using templates). Glue the shoe upper centrally to the cream card with spray adhesive.

2 Cut the shoe lining from light blue paper and the heel from yellow ochre paper. Cut the shoe trim from gold paper, cutting along the lower edge with fancy-edged scissors. Glue the pieces to the shoe with spray adhesive.

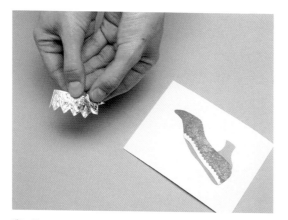

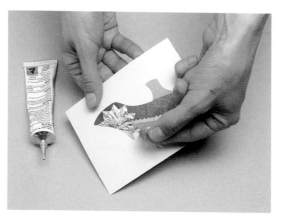

3 Cut a strip of gold crêpe paper 6 x 2cm (2½ x ¾in) for the ruffle, cutting the short edges parallel with the grain of the paper. Cut a zig-zag edge along one long edge. Gather up the long, straight edge between your fingers, forming a rosette, and stick a piece of adhesive tape underneath to hold the gathers in place.

4 Glue the ruffle to the front of the shoe with all-purpose household glue. Cut the tip off a pink marabou feather, dab the end with glue and poke it into position behind the ruffle.

5 Cut a 1cm (⅜in) diameter circle of pink metallic card and glue it to the centre of the rosette. Using spray adhesive, glue the picture centrally to a 14 x 10.5cm (5¾ x 4¼in) rectangle of ribbed gold paper.

6 Cut a 34 x 13.5cm (13½ x 5½in) rectangle of gold card with a craft knife, metal ruler and cutting mat. Score across the centre with a bone folder or craft knife and fold the card in half. Cut a template of the frame from scrap paper and use the template to draw around the notches on the card front. Cut out the notches then stick the picture to the front with spray adhesive.

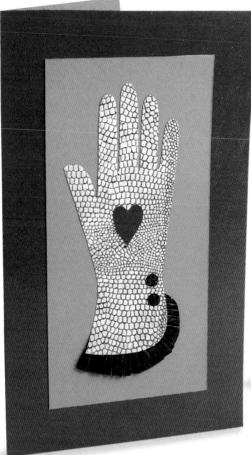

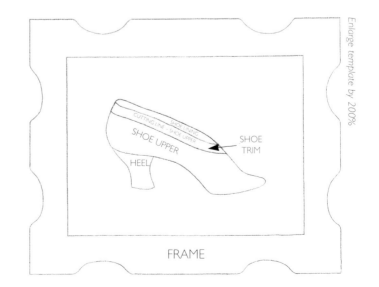

Handbag Card

Cut the bag from thick white paper, then fold the flap over the front. Make zebra-stripe stickers from textured black paper and apply. Cut the ends of a strip of red leatherette paper in a curve, pleat and glue under the bag flap. For the handle, plait three lengths of red leatherette paper and glue the ends behind the bag. The clasp and background is gold crocodile-effect paper.

Glove Card

Cut the glove from snakeskin-effect paper, and the heart and red background from leatherette paper. The frilled cuff, glued under the edge of the glove, is made from pleated crocodile-effect paper, and the buttons are circles of the same paper.

CUTTING LINE — SHOE LINING — SHOE UPPER

SHOE UPPER

HEEL

SHOE TRIM

FRAME

Enlarge template by 200%

Dazzling Metallics

Tantalizing shiny papers give a sense of glamour to gift cards. Plain metallic card and paper is readily available and shiny gift-wrapping papers with fancy finishes are often inexpensive to buy. Unusual holographic films are sometimes sticky-backed so can be applied easily to card to strengthen them.

Gift cards do not have to be square or rectangular – this pair of shimmering cards are topped with elaborate curls, while different textures of metallic papers and cards decorate the fronts.

YOU WILL NEED

Blue and red holographic film
White card
Craft knife, metal ruler and cutting mat
Bone folder (optional)
Metallic paper – copper, pink, gold,
    red and blue

Metallic blue card
Spray adhesive
Double-sided tape 2.5cm (1in) wide

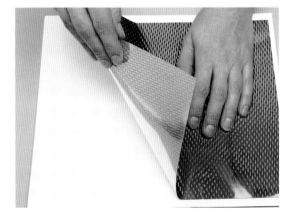

1 Peel the backing paper off a piece of blue holographic film and stick the film smoothly to white card. Use the template provided here to cut the gift card with a craft knife, resting on a cutting mat. Score along the broken line with a bone folder or craft knife.

2 Cut a 12 x 6.5cm (4¾ x 2½in) rectangle of metallic copper paper and a 11 x 5.5cm (4½ x 2¼in) rectangle of metallic blue card. Stick the large copper rectangle to the front of the card, then stick the smaller blue rectangle on top with spray adhesive.

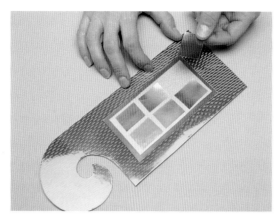

3 Cut three rectangles of metallic copper and metallic pink paper freehand with a pair of scissors to fit on the blue rectangle. Arrange the pieces on the card front, alternating the colours and glue in place with spray adhesive.

4 Apply 2.5cm (1in) wide double-sided adhesive tape to the wrong side of pieces of gold, metallic pink, red and blue papers. Draw three eggs on the backing paper of the gold and pink metallic papers. Draw three circles on the backing papers of the red and blue metallic papers and holographic film.

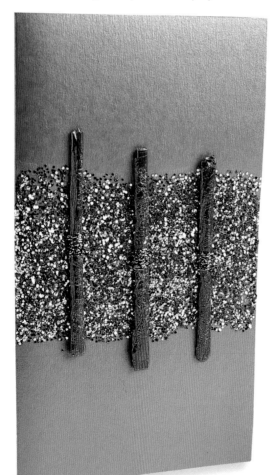

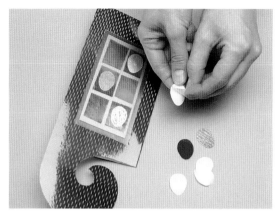

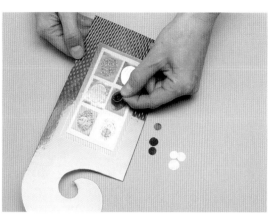

5 Cut out the shapes. Peel the backing tapes off the eggs and stick the gold eggs on the pink rectangles and the pink eggs on the copper rectangles.

6 Peel the backing tapes and papers from the circles and stick the red circles to the gold eggs and blue circles to the pink eggs.

Scroll Card

For this stylish card, sprinkle sequin dust on a broad band of PVA glue. Roll metallic foil sweet papers into three logs and place upright on the card front, oversewing them in place with metallic thread.

Crown Card

The metallic-paper crown is applied to the card with adhesive foam. White sequin dust is sprinkled on a band of PVA glue. Rolled and coiled metallic foil sweet papers decorate the crown, and metallic plastic shapes are glued along the top of the card.

Enlarge template by 200%

Paint Resist

Masking fluid is a very versatile medium that can be applied to areas that you do not want to be painted. The fluid dries quickly then paint is applied on top. Once the paint has dried, the masking fluid is simply rubbed away to reveal the unpainted paper beneath.

The earth-toned patterns on this rustic gift card are inspired by African textiles. Using masking fluid will retain the definition of the design beneath the paint. The use of raffia and a twig continue the natural feel of the card.

YOU WILL NEED

A5 sheet of brown handmade
   writing paper
Artist's paintbrush
Masking fluid
Acrylic paints – dark brown,
   chestnut brown and cream

Two A5 sheets of beige handmade
   writing paper
Bone folder (optional)
Craft knife (optional)
Large needle
Raffia and twig

1 Use the template provided to draw the design on a sheet of brown writing paper with a pencil. Now paint the design with masking fluid, painting simple patterns within the rectangles. Leave the fluid to dry. Allow the paintbrush to dry then pull the dried masking fluid off the bristles.

2 Paint the design with acrylic paints in shades of brown, blending the colours together on the paper. Work quickly – there is no need to be precise. Paint a 1.2cm (½in) wide border around the outer edges with dark brown paint, then leave to dry.

3 Rub off the masking fluid with a finger, rubbing along the lines with a circular motion. When all the masking fluid has been removed, tear the outer edges of the brown paper against a ruler along the centre of the dark brown painted border, following the instructions on page 14.

4 Using two beige sheets of handmade writing paper (for the front and back of the card) score a margin 3.5cm (1½in) in from the short left-hand edge of both sheets with a bone folder or craft knife.

5 Thread a needle with a length of raffia and knot the end. Position the painted design on the card front and secure it in place with a few stitches along the top and lower edges. Knot the raffia ends on the underside and cut off the excess.

6 Place the front of the card on the back, hold a twig on the margin and over-sew it with raffia, knotting the ends on the back of the card.

Mini Pattern Cards

Elements of the large pattern are used on these small cards. The backgrounds to the cards are sheets of handmade A5 paper folded in half. A running stitch worked in raffia provides a finishing touch.

Guinea Fowl Card

Paint resist is used again for this delightful card. An A4 sheet of handmade paper is folded in half to form the background to the guinea fowl design. A row of tiny pebbles is glued below the design.

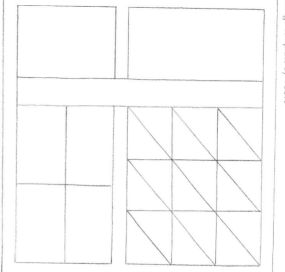

Enlarge template by 133%

53

Three-dimensional Pot Plants

This perky plant in its own pot is not only a three-dimensional gift card but is also the ultimate low-maintenance houseplant for a not so green-fingered friend. Make a box envelope (see page 19) to contain and protect the card.

A pretty daisy in a terracotta pot will look great gracing a sunny window-sill. A message can be written on the back of the pot before it is constructed or written on a luggage label and fastened to the stem.

YOU WILL NEED

Craft knife, metal ruler and cutting mat
Terracotta card
Bone folder (optional)

Paper – white, yellow and lime green
Double-sided tape 2.5cm (1in) wide
All-purpose household glue

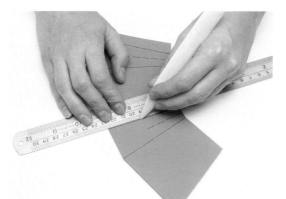

1 Use the template to cut the pot from terracotta card. Mark the solid and broken lines on the wrong side. Score along the solid lines with a bone folder or craft knife. Fold along the scored lines then open out flat again. Write your message now on the back of the pot if you wish.

2 Cut the flower from white paper using the largest flower template. Cut the petals to the flower centre. Apply double-sided adhesive tape to the wrong side of a piece of yellow paper and cut out the flower centre. Peel off the backing tape and stick to the centre of the flower.

3 Pull the petals gently between your fingers to curl them. Cut the stem from lime green card. Stick the flower to the top of the stem with double-sided tape.

4 Score along the broken lines on the stem base with a bone folder or craft knife. Apply double-sided tape to the tabs on the stem and pot on the right side. Fold the stem base tabs backwards and peel off the backing tapes. Stick the stem base tabs to the wrong side of the pot sides, matching the broken lines.

5 Peel the backing tape off the end tab of the pot and stick the tab under the opposite edge of the pot.

6 Using the template provided, cut the brim from terracotta card. Score along the solid lines with a bone folder or craft knife, then fold along the scored lines. Run a line of all-purpose glue along the upper long edge of the pot and, starting at the tab end, stick the brim around the top of the pot, matching the upper edges.

Stone Plant Pot Card
This pot is cut from textured white card, but the brim has been omitted to imitate a rustic stone planter.

Chrysanthemum Card
A large, medium and small flower have been cut from purple paper using the flower template and stuck one on top of the other to create a jaunty chrysanthemum. Cut the pot with a scalloped edge.

POT BRIM

TAB

POT

END TAB

STEM

TAB

TAB

Enlarge templates by 200%

57

Stencilled Zodiac Signs

Sending a horoscope-inspired gift card shows you have given thought to the recipient's birth date and chosen a suitable motif to mark the occasion. Stencilling is a very popular craft because extremely professional results are achieved so quickly and easily.

Stencilling is an ideal medium for the zodiac and the type of paper and card that you work on can convey the nature of the star sign.

YOU WILL NEED

Stencil sheet
Masking tape
Craft knife, metal ruler
   and cutting mat
Textured black paper

Acrylic paints – salmon
   pink and brown
Ceramic tile
Flat paintbrush
Light brown card

Bone folder (optional)
Black thonging
Chestnut brown paper
Hole punch
Large needle

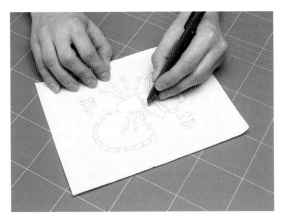

1 First, draw the template on paper. Then tape a piece of stencil sheet on top and, resting on a cutting mat, cut out the cut-outs with a craft knife. Remove the stencil.

2 Tape the stencil to a piece of textured black paper, then tape over the symbols. With a flat paintbrush, put some salmon pink paint on to a ceramic tile. Dab at the paint with a stencil brush and, holding the brush upright, stencil the scorpion, moving the brush in a circular motion. Leave to dry.

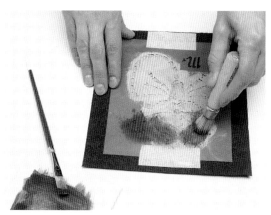

3 Remove the tape from the symbols. Put some brown paint on to the ceramic tile with a flat paintbrush. Stencil the symbols and just the outer edges of the scorpion with the brown paint. Leave to dry, then remove the stencil. Tear away the paper in an irregular shape around the design.

4 Tear two 20cm (8in) squares of light brown card for the front and back, as on page 14. Score a margin across the squares 2.5cm (1in) in from the left-hand side with a bone folder or craft knife. Position the design on the card front. Make two holes in one corner of the black paper with a large needle and two corresponding holes on the front. Lace with black thonging to hold the paper to the card, knotting the ends together on the underside of the card. Repeat at each corner.

5 Tear two 19cm (7½in) squares of chestnut brown paper for inserts. Position the papers inside the front and back with the left-hand edges level.

6 Punch a pair of holes centrally on the margin through all the thicknesses of the card. Thread with thonging, then knot the ends together. Fold the front open along the scored line then close again.

Leo Card

A regal lion head is stencilled with gold acrylic paint on to red paper. Soft gold paper is scrunched tightly then flattened again and applied to red card with spray adhesive. Use the Leo zodiac sign template on page 63.

Aquarius Card

An amphora of water in shades of blue and lilac is stencilled on to blue card using pearlized paints. The card is roughly torn to a rectangle and applied with spray adhesive to a mottled blue and white card. Use the Aquarius zodiac sign template on page 62.

AQUARIUS 21 January – 19 February

PISCES 20 February – 20 March

ARIES 21 March – 20 April

TAURUS 21 April – 21 May

GEMINI 22 May – 21 June

CANCER 22 June – 23 July

LEO 24 July – 23 August

VIRGO 24 August – 23 September

LIBRA 24 September – 23 October

SCORPIO 24 October – 22 November

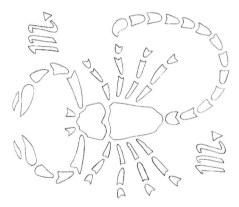

SAGITTARIUS 23 November – 21 December

CAPRICORN 22 December – 20 January

Enlarge templates by 200%

63

Mixed Media

Gift cards can be decorated with some wonderful, unexpected materials – almost anything can be used as long as it is not too heavy and would tip the card over or come unattached. If fragile three-dimensional materials are used, remember to package the card well (see pages 18 and 19 for padded and box envelopes).

Balsa wood and found driftwood are simple to cut and, being lightweight, they are easy to glue to a card and yet have the appearance of a weightier wood. Fine metal and wire are unusual materials for card making and great effects can be achieved very easily. Craft shops sell fine metals for embossing and wires in various thicknesses intended for making jewellery.

Fabrics and haberdashery components have a multitude of applications and, again, are lightweight and can be glued easily (see Techniques, page 13 for advice on glues). All-purpose household glue is a very versatile adhesive. PVA is good for sticking pressed flowers and many other materials. Use a plastic spreader or strip of card to apply an even covering of adhesive. A cocktail stick is useful for applying a tiny dab of glue.

If you practise other crafts, they may well lend themselves to card making. Small carved and modelled wooden and clay motifs can be glued to a card. Embroidery, silk painting and fabric collage also go hand in hand with making gift cards. Creating a gift card with a craft that is new to you is a good introduction to the technique and if you enjoy it, you can take it further. Gilding is a fine example, as to gild a complex three-dimensional item may be daunting to a beginner but working on a small scale on paper may inspire you to tackle a larger object.

Gather together unusual materials such as fine metals, eye-catching sequins and lengths of wire.

Balsa Wood

Balsa wood is a very versatile material. It is inexpensive to buy from model and craft shops and is easy to cut with a craft knife. The wood comes in sheet form and rods of different thicknesses. It can be left unpainted for simplicity, richly painted or given a quick, subtle wash of colour depending on the effect you want.

This bobbing wooden boat would make a lovely bon voyage card. It has tiny portholes made from metal eyelets and sails on a fabric sea. A row of small shells suggest a shoreline.

You Will Need

Balsa wood 5mm (¼in) thick
Craft knife and cutting mat
Acrylic paints – cream, red and blue
Artist's paintbrush
Three 5mm (¼in) chrome eyelets
White card
White woven-effect paper

Spray adhesive
Bone folder (optional)
Fine-weave blue fabric
Vilene Bondaweb
Three small shells
All-purpose household glue

1 Cut the boat template from scrap paper and draw around it on balsa wood with a pencil. Cut out the boat with a craft knife, resting on a cutting mat.

2 Draw the cabin porthole and cabin line on the boat with a pencil, pressing hard to make an indentation.

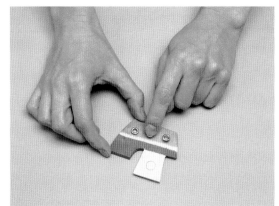

3 Thin some cream acrylic paint with water, paint the cabin and leave to dry. Thin red paint with water and paint a band across the top of the boat (see main photograph). Thin the blue paint and paint a band 5mm (¼ in) below the red band: the two colours of the thinned paints will spread toward each other. Leave to dry.

4 Place the eyelets in a row on the boat and press them into the wood. Apply white woven-effect paper to white card with spray adhesive and cut a 21 x 16cm (8½ x 6½ in) rectangle for the card. Score across the centre with a bone folder or craft knife and fold in half.

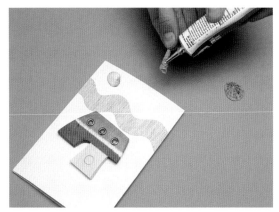

5 Use the wave template to draw the wave on the paper backing of a piece of Bondaweb, then refer to the technique on page 14 to apply the Bondaweb to fine-weave blue fabric. Peel off the backing paper and apply the wave across the card front. Cut off the excess fabric at each side of the card.

6 Glue the boat to the card at a jaunty angle, then use an all-purpose glue to stick the shells in a row along the lower edge.

Bird-house Card

This trio of colour-washed bird-houses are cut from 5mm (¼in) thick balsa wood. A metal eyelet pressed into each house provides an entrance. The roof is a 4.5cm x 5mm (1¾ x ¼in) strip of corrugated card glued over the gable top. The bird-houses are then glued to a tall, narrow card that has a strip of torn paper along the opening edge.

BOAT

WAVE

Enlarge templates by 200%

Christmas Tree Card

Lengths of fine wooden dowelling are arranged tree fashion on the card front and oversewn at the intersections. A strip of torn paper is applied along the lower edge. A quirky heart and star cut from 2mm (⅛in) thick balsa wood are washed with red paint and glued to the card.

69

Embossed Metal

Fine metal, which is available in sheet form from craft shops, is easy to emboss with a ballpoint pen (an old dried-up pen will do). Simple motifs are the most effective and can be highlighted with glass paints, their transparency allowing the metal to shine through.

This amusing gift card of sardines in a tin is ideal for this medium, the metal being similar to the tin container and shiny like the fish. Cut the metal with an old pair of scissors as the metal will blunt a new pair.

YOU WILL NEED

Tracing paper
Sheet of fine aluminium
Masking tape
Kitchen paper towels
Ballpoint pen
Glass paints – red, turquoise and grey
Artist's paintbrushes

Dark green tissue paper
Grey card
Craft knife, metal ruler and cutting mat
Bone folder (optional)
PVA glue
All-purpose household glue

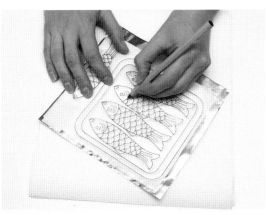

1 Trace the fishes and sardine tin template on to tracing paper and tape it to a sheet of fine aluminium. Resting on a few sheets of kitchen paper towels, redraw the whole design along the outlines, pressing hard with a ballpoint pen to emboss the metal.

2 Remove the tracing and turn the design over. Using glass paints, paint the tin red, the details on the fish turquoise, and the mouths and eyes grey. Leave the paints to dry then use an old pair of scissors to cut out the tin and fish.

3 Cut a 20cm (8in) square of dark green tissue paper. Fold this vertically into eighths and cut horizontally into strips 3mm (⅛in) wide. Pull apart the shredded pieces.

4 Cut a rectangle of grey card 24 x 12cm (9½ x 4¾in) with a craft knife, metal ruler and cutting mat. Score across the centre with a bone folder or craft knife and fold in half. Apply PVA glue to the card front, using a scrap of card to spread it evenly. Arrange the shredded tissue on top and press down flat. Cut off the excess tissue just inside the outer edges.

5 Glue the sardine tin to the card front with all-purpose household glue. Arrange the five fish on the shredded tissue, overlapping them within the tin, then glue them in place.

6 Carefully cut the card around the curved edges of the tin with scissors – use an old pair of scissors, as cutting metal will blunt the scissor blades.

Fossil Card

An ammonite fossil is embossed on a square of fine copper metal then glued to the front of a card of thick handmade paper. Lines embossed on the metal are cut into narrow strips and glued above and below the square as borders.

Feather Card

A feather is embossed on a rectangle of sheet copper then glued to hessian. The fabric is frayed around the edges then glued to a card of thin handmade paper that has been glued to red card for support.

Enlarge template by 200%

Wire Work

Unusual cards can be created by bending simple shapes from glistening wire to form bold designs. There are masses of types of wire to use. Jewellery wire from craft shops and bonsai wire from garden centres are easy to bend and are available in different thicknesses. Use fuse wire to fix wire designs in place.

A whimsical reindeer fashioned from copper wire stands proudly on this Christmas card. A heart cut from a sheet of fine metal has a quick and realistic verdigris effect applied.

YOU WILL NEED

Copper wire
   1mm/(⅛in) diameter
Pliers
Metal snips
One red bead with
   large hole
Sheet of fine copper
Ceramic tile

Flat paintbrush
Acrylic paints –
    aquamarine and black
Natural sponge
Needle
Fine copper wire
White card

Cream-striped tissue
   paper
Spray adhesive
Craft knife, metal ruler
   and cutting mat
Bone folder (optional)
Fine artist's paintbrush

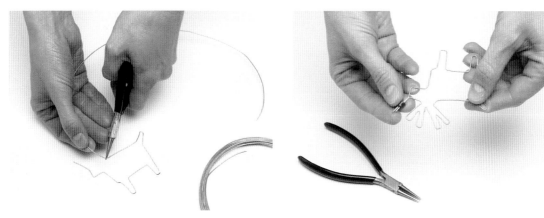

1 Using the reindeer template as a guide, bend the copper wire into the reindeer shape with a pair of pliers, holding it against the template from time to time to check the shape. Snip off the excess wire.

2 Insert the ends of the wire through the red bead, then bend the wire ends to the back of the bead with a pair of pliers to hold it in place and snip off the excess wire.

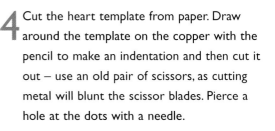

3 Apply a thin film of aquamarine acrylic paint to a ceramic tile with a flat paintbrush. Dab at the paint with a moistened natural sponge then dab the paint on to the copper, resting on scrap paper, to produce a verdigris effect. Leave to dry.

4 Cut the heart template from paper. Draw around the template on the copper with the pencil to make an indentation and then cut it out – use an old pair of scissors, as cutting metal will blunt the scissor blades. Pierce a hole at the dots with a needle.

5 Insert a length of fine copper wire through the right side of the heart through the top hole and out of the lower hole. Apply cream-striped tissue paper to white card with spray adhesive. Cut a rectangle of this covered card 20 x 13cm (8 x 5in) using a craft knife and metal ruler, resting on a cutting mat. Score across the centre with a bone folder or craft knife and fold in half.

6 Open the card out flat. Lay the reindeer centrally on the card front with the heart in the centre. Pierce a hole just above and below the centre of the body. Thread the fine wires attached to the heart through the holes and twist the ends together inside the card. Dot the eye with black paint.

Bound Stone Card
Here, a plain card has a layer
of metallic paper applied as a
background to a lucky gemstone.
The gemstone is applied to a scrap
of card with fine, gold-coloured
jewellery wire. The wire ends are
twisted together on the underside of
the card piece, which is then glued
to front of the card.

Spiral card
Copper wire is bound into a spiral
and a heart-shaped drop bead is
suspended in the centre to make
this understated valentine greetings
card. The top of the spiral is fixed
to the centre of the card front
with fine copper wire.

Templates shown actual size

77

Gilding

Luxurious effects can be achieved by using transfer gold leaf, where the fine metal is applied to the card over gold size. The gold size and transfer gold leaf, which come in sheets with a paper backing, are available from art shops.

This dramatic card is ideal for many celebrations such as weddings, anniversaries and Christmas. A golden harp has strings of fine gold thread and the front and back of the card are laced together with gossamer-thin organza ribbon.

YOU WILL NEED

Thick white handmade paper
Artist's paintbrush
Bone folder or craft knife
Gold size (15 minute)
One sheet of transfer Dutch metal
    gold leaf

Soft brush
Gold embroidery thread
Hole punch
Cream organza ribbon 40cm (16in)
    of 2.5cm (1in) wide

1 Tear two 18cm (7¼in) squares of thick white handmade paper for the front and back (see instructions on page 14). Score a margin 2.5cm (1in) in from the left-hand side with a bone folder or craft knife. Cut the harp template from scrap paper and trace around it lightly with a pencil on the card front.

2 With a paintbrush, apply gold size to the inside of the harp outline, and set aside for fifteen minutes to dry.

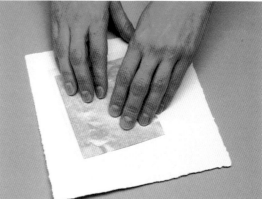

3 Cut a piece of transfer gold leaf slightly larger than the harp. When the size feels tacky, lay the gold leaf face down on top and gently press in place.

Pressed Flower Card
A broad sweep of silver leaf has been applied to textured card. Three delicate, pressed flower heads are stuck on top in a row using an all-purpose household glue.

Pressed Leaf Card
Here, gold leaf has been applied to a pressed autumn leaf then a little red acrylic paint has been brushed on and rubbed off immediately with a kitchen towel to enhance the colour. The leaf is glued to paper impregnated with metallic bits, stuck on to card to stiffen it.

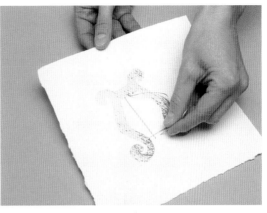

4 Sweep away the excess gold leaf with a soft brush. If the gold leaf has not adhered in places, simply press a piece of the left-over gold leaf on the gap.

5 Pierce holes on the harp at the ends of the 'string' lines (three at the top and three at the bottom and one either side). Thread a needle with gold thread and knot the end. Sew the thread in and out of the holes to form the strings, then knot the thread securely on the underside.

6 Lay the front of the card on the back and punch a pair of holes centrally through the margin. Thread with the cream organza ribbon and knot the ends together. Cut the ribbon ends diagonally. Fold the front open along the scored line then close again.

Template shown actual size

Painted Silk

Silk painting is a highly popular craft. The rich effect of paint flowed over silk is very easy to achieve and always looks stunning.

As can be seen by this card, the flowing lines of Celtic designs lend themselves very well to silk painting. To accentuate the luxurious colouring of this stylized bird, a bead-trimmed cord was added and the gift card has a formal insert inside.

YOU WILL NEED

Tracing paper
White haboutai silk
   22cm (8¾in) square
Masking tape
Embroidery hoop
   15cm (6in) diameter
Gold silk outliner (gutta)

Silk paints – red, wine,
   yellow, beige and black
Artist's paintbrush
Tissue paper
Red card
Craft knife, metal ruler and
   cutting mat

Bone folder (optional)
White paper
Spray adhesive
Glue stick
Gold cord 1.2m (1½yd)
Gold and red beads
   with large holes

1 Trace the bird design on to tracing paper. Tape the silk on top with masking tape and then trace the design lightly on to the silk with a pencil. Stretch the silk in an embroidery hoop, placing the design in the centre.

2 Redraw the design on the silk with gold silk outliner, starting at the centre of the design and working outwards so that you do not smudge the outliner. Leave to dry. Check to see if any of the lines do not join up or are very thin. If so, go over them again so that one silk paint colour will not be able to seep into the next.

3 Dip the paintbrush in the red silk paint. Press the brush into the centre of one of the areas to be painted red: the paint will flow within the outline. Add more paint if necessary until the shape is filled. Refer to the main photograph to fill in all the red areas. Clean the brush with water then fill in all the other colours. When dry, remove from the hoop and press the silk between two layers of tissue paper.

4 Cut a rectangle of red card 30 x 20cm (12 x 8in) using a craft knife and metal ruler, resting on a cutting mat. Score across the centre with a bone folder or craft knife and fold in half. Roughly cut out the silk picture, leaving a margin all round. Glue it to white paper with spray adhesive. Now cut out close to the outer edges of the outliner so the silk does not fray, then stick to the card front with spray adhesive.

5 Cut a rectangle of white paper 29 x 19cm (11 1/4 x 7 1/4in) for the insert. Fold the paper in half. Use a glue stick to run a line of glue close to the fold and slip the insert inside the gift card.

6 Bend the length of gold cord in half and slip it inside the card with the fold at the top. Pull the ends to the outside through the loop. Slip a few gold and red beads on each end then knot the cord under the beads and cut off the excess.

Enlarge template by 133%

Bookmark Card

This bookmark design has been applied to card with spray adhesive then cut out. Two slits are cut in a card front to insert the ends of the bookmark into. A border has been drawn on the card front with gold outliner.

Triangle Card

Thick, textured black paper has been applied to red card with spray adhesive to provide an impressive background to this graphic Celtic knot. The painted silk design is stuck to plain white paper with spray adhesive, then cut out and glued to the card front.

Transparent Fabrics

Just a few snippets of lovely iridescent organza fabrics are needed to create delicate-looking gift cards. Try out your embroidery skills with a few easy but effective stitches on a tiered celebration cake to commemorate a wedding or a special anniversary.

YOU WILL NEED

Vilene Bondaweb
Scrap of gold organza
Cream stranded cotton
  (floss) pearlized
  embroidery thread
Embroidery needle

White card
Silver metallic stranded
  embroidery thread
Finely textured ochre-
  coloured paper
Spray adhesive

Craft knife, metal ruler
  and cutting mat
Bone folder (optional)
All-purpose household
  glue
Four silver bugle beads
Cherub-shaped sequin

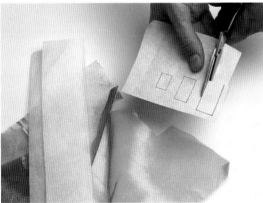

1 Draw the cake tiers on the paper side of the Bondaweb – the sizes are 3 x 2cm (1¼ x ¾in), 2.5 x 1.5 (1 x ½in) and 1.5 x 1cm (½ x ¼in). Apply the tiers to the gold organza (see instructions on page 14) and cut out. Peel off the paper backing.

2 Embroider the motifs with one strand of cream embroidery thread in backstitch using the main picture as a guide for positioning.

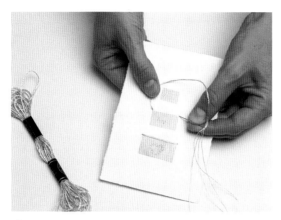

3 Tear a rectangle of white card 13 x 9cm (5¼ x 3¾in). Arrange the tiers on top and bond them in place with an iron. Using four strands of silver embroidery thread, stitch a straight stitch across the top of each tier.

4 Using three strands of cream embroidery thread, work a row of French knots along the top of each tier. Work a single knot in the centre of the top tier.

5 Glue ochre-coloured paper to white card with spray adhesive. Cut a rectangle 28 x 18cm (11 x 7in). Score across the centre with a bone folder or craft knife and fold in half. Glue the embroidered panel to the centre of the front with spray adhesive.

6 Use an all-purpose glue to stick silver bugle beads between the tiers as columns. Glue a sequin cherub to the top of the cake. You could sprinkle more cherubs inside the card as a surprise to the recipients when they open it!

Christmas Tree Card

Tear a rectangle of strong tracing paper to make this filmy Christmas card. Fold in half and spray glue two roughly cut rectangles of organza to the front, one on top of the other. Glue a Christmas tree on top with Bondaweb. A tiny sequin star tops the tree.

Pomander Card

This fragrant greetings card is also a gift. The pomander is suspended from the card with ribbon so it can be removed easily. To make the pomander, cut three hearts of increasing size from three different scraps of metallic organza using pinking shears. Layer the hearts and stitch together, sandwiching lavender flowers under the top layer. Add a ribbon rose and sew the heart to a length of fine ribbon. Punch a pair of holes at the top of the card front and tie the ribbon through the holes.

Button Collage

A few buttons are a lovely addition to a gift card, giving a three-dimensional, tactile effect. Herald a new baby with a pretty greetings card showing a row of white nappies on a washing line blowing in a blustery breeze.

The nappies are fixed on with tiny, toy-making buttons but small buttons for babies clothing would also be suitable.

YOU WILL NEED

Pale blue card
Craft knife, metal ruler and cutting mat
Acrylic paints – white and green
Ceramic tile
Flat paintbrush
Natural sponge
Scrap of white fabric

Thick cream thread
All-purpose household glue
Cocktail stick
Six tiny blue or pink buttons
White card
Bone folder (optional)
Spray adhesive

1 Cut a rectangle of pale blue card 15.5 x 10cm (6¼ x 4in) using a craft knife and metal ruler, resting on a cutting mat. Apply a thin film of white acrylic paint to a ceramic tile with a flat paintbrush.

2 Rest the blue card on a piece of scrap paper. Dab at the paint with a moistened natural sponge then dab the paint on to the top half of the card in two patches to create two clouds. Leave to dry.

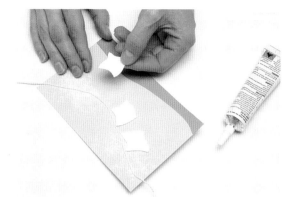

3 With a flat paintbrush, apply a broad sweep of green acrylic paint across the bottom of the card to suggest hills. Leave to dry.

4 Using the template provided, cut out the nappies from white fabric. Arrange a length of thick cream thread across the card as a washing line (check the position of the nappies). Use glue to fix the ends of the 'washing line' to the back of the card. Carefully glue the washing line in position on the card front by applying the glue sparingly with a cocktail stick.

5 Replace the nappies and glue them in place. Glue a button at each upper corner of a nappy, using a cocktail stick to apply the glue. Cut white card 27 x 18.5cm (10$^1/_2$ x 7$^1/_4$ in). Score across the centre with a bone folder or craft knife and fold in half.

6 Cut out the scallop template from scrap paper, place it along the lower edge of the card and draw around the scallops. Use a craft knife to cut away the scallops, resting on a cutting mat. Glue the picture to the front of the greetings card with spray adhesive.

Flower Card

Raid the sewing box for a scrap of gold cord and a mother-of-pearl button. The flower motif is traced on to tracing paper and taped by one edge to the card front with masking tape. The cord is stuck down using all-purpose household glue. By flipping the tracing back and forth over the design, the cord can be glued accurately. The button is glued in the centre to finish.

Heart Card

Spray glue two layers of handmade paper together. Cut the card edges with fancy-edged scissors. A single layer of mother-of-pearl buttons is glued in a heart shape on the front with all-purpose household glue. Extra buttons are glued on top to fill the gaps.

Enlarge templates by 133%

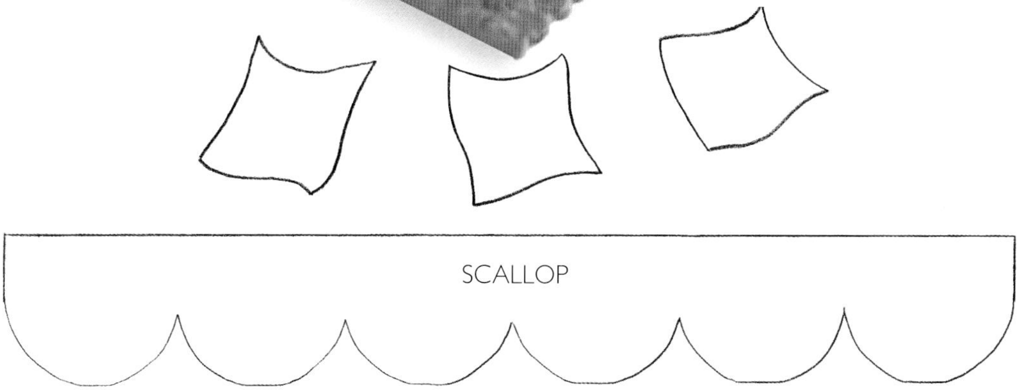

SCALLOP

93

Beads and Sequins

*Just a few small beads and sequins applied to a gift card will give it an
exotic touch and will catch the light when displayed.*

*Christmas cards are usually hung at the festive season so why not make
a card and a decoration as one. Glistening baubles cut from coloured
card take on a three-dimensional look when decorated with shiny beads
and sequins.*

YOU WILL NEED

Red card
Craft knife, metal ruler and
 cutting mat
Scrap of gold card
Double-sided tape 2.5cm (1in) wide
String of sequins

All-purpose household glue
Bugle beads
Large jump ring
Gold thread

1 Use a bauble template to cut a bauble
from red card with a craft knife, resting on
a cutting mat. Lightly draw lines across the
bauble with a pencil. It is best to write your
message on the back of the card now as once
the beads are stuck on the front it will make
the surface uneven for writing.

2 Stick a piece of double-sided adhesive tape
to the wrong side of gold card and cut out
the holder. Peel off the backing tape and stick
the holder to the top of the bauble.

3 Cut a length of sequin string to stick along one drawn line, gluing the thread ends to the underside of the sequins so they do not unravel. Run a line of glue along the pencil line and fix the sequins in place. Repeat on one or two other lines.

4 Run a line of glue along a pencil line and stick bugle beads end to end along the line. Repeat on some of the other lines too.

5 Run a line of glue just below another line and place bugle beads upright side by side on the glue, nudging the beads into place with the tip of a pencil. Now slip a few sequins off the string and glue them singly to the bauble.

6 Pierce a hole through the holder with a needle. Gently pull open a jump-ring and slip it through the hole. Close the ring then thread a length of gold thread through it. Knot the thread ends together.

Pink Sequin Leaf Card
Three 3cm (1¼ in) squares of red silk are applied to the front of a card with Bondaweb. A large gold sequin is glued to each square with a leaf-shaped sequin glued on top. Organza ribbon is stuck along the card with double-sided adhesive tape and a string of sequins is glued on top of this.

Blue Sequin Leaf Card
On this elegant card, a 4cm (1½ in) wide strip of Bondaweb is applied to striped silk. The fabric is cut 1cm (⅜ in) wider each side of the Bondaweb and then frayed, and applied to the front of a card. A row of leaf-shaped sequins, shiny red ribbon and a row of purple bugle beads are stuck to the fabric.

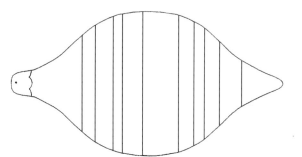

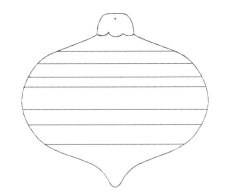

Enlarge templates by 200%

97

Organic Materials

The natural world is a wonderful source of materials. From the kitchen try eggshells, cloves and bay leaves. Collect flowers and leaves from the garden, to press between sheets of kitchen towel within the pages of a heavy book.

This Easter card with its broken eggshell worked in a mosaic of little fragments is quite quick to make. The egg is set on layers of handmade papers in subtle, coordinating colours.

YOU WILL NEED

One duck egg
Pink handmade paper
PVA glue
Scrap of card or glue spreader
Craft knife
Cream handmade paper
Spray adhesive

Textured lilac card
Bone folder (optional)
Thick needle
Natural linen thread
Bradawl (optional)
White feather
All-purpose household glue

1 Crack the egg and keep the contents for cooking. Pull away the membrane inside the shell and discard it, then wash and dry the shell. Roughly tear an 11 x 8cm (4½ x 3¼in) rectangle of pink handmade paper by tearing the paper between your fingers.

2 Using the egg template provided, draw the broken egg on the pink rectangle lightly with a pencil. Break off pieces of the shell – about 1.5cm (⅝in) diameter pieces are a good size. Use a thin strip of card or a glue spreader to spread all-purpose glue evenly on about one third of one drawn section.

3 Place a piece of shell on the glue. Press the shell with your fingers to break it into smaller pieces.

4 Use the tip of a craft knife to separate and spread the fragments apart. Work quickly before the glue dries, then repeat all over the drawn shell sections, keeping within the outlines to define the shapes. Set aside to dry.

5 Tear a rectangle of cream handmade paper by hand, slightly larger than the pink rectangle. Glue the pink rectangle on the cream rectangle with spray adhesive. Now tear a rectangle of textured lilac card 27 x 18cm (11 x 7in) following the instructions on page 14. Score across the centre with a bone folder or craft knife, then fold the card in half. Place the picture horizontally on the front of the card.

6 Thread a thick needle with linen thread and attach the picture to the card front with a few stitches, knotting the thread ends securely on the underside of the card. Use a bradawl to make the holes if necessary. Glue a tiny white feather between the shell halves.

Shell Card

When using shells for making cards, choose small or flat shells so they are not too difficult to pack for sending. Here, a flat shell, a feather, a pressed leaf and some petals are glued to torn papers with PVA glue.

Bay Leaves Card

Bay leaves, pressed flowers and a row of cloves are stuck to colourful torn papers with PVA glue. A pretty postage stamp gives an interesting change of texture.

Template shown actual size

Folk Fabric Scraps

Recycled fabric oddments make wonderful folk-style gift cards. Only tiny scraps of fabric are needed but they will give a comforting, homespun feel to your creations.

This happy angel is holding an armful of hearts. Her arms and legs are made from cord, simple knots suggest the hands and feet and her hair is made from a strip of knotted fabric.

YOU WILL NEED

Natural white cord
Yellow fabric
Raffia
Masking tape
Scrap of cream card
Red and black coloured
    pencils

Scrap of calico
White corrugated card
Craft knife, metal ruler
    and cutting mat
Bright green fabric
Spray adhesive

All-purpose household
    glue
Brown fabric
Scraps of brown
    corrugated card, gold
    card and thick
    handmade paper

1 Cut two 15cm (6in) lengths of natural white cord for the legs and a rectangle of yellow fabric 14.5 x 6cm (5¾ x 2⅜in) for the dress. Place the dress centrally on the legs with the top ends of the legs and one long edge of the dress level. Tie raffia around the top of the dress and legs about 1.5cm (⅝in) below the upper edge.

2 Tie a knot in each leg 8cm (3¼in) below the tied raffia and cut off the cord below the knots.

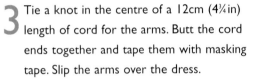

3 Tie a knot in the centre of a 12cm (4¾in) length of cord for the arms. Butt the cord ends together and tape them with masking tape. Slip the arms over the dress.

4 Draw the head on cream card using the template supplied. Draw the facial features with red and black coloured pencils and cut out the head. Cut the wings from calico using the template.

5 Cut white corrugated card 28 x 18.5cm (11 x 7¼in), cutting the short edges parallel with the corrugations. Fold the card in half. Cut a 14.5 x 12cm (5¾ x 4¾in) rectangle of bright green fabric and fray all the edges for 5mm (¼in). Stick the fabric centrally to the front of the card with spray adhesive. Arrange the angel and head on the fabric, on the wings.

6 Glue the pieces in place with all-purpose adhesive. Cut a 1cm (⅜in) wide strip of brown fabric and tie three knots in it, 2.5cm (1in) apart. Cut 5mm (¼in) each side of the knots and glue them around the head as hair. Using the template, cut three hearts from brown corrugated card, gold card and thick handmade paper and glue these in the angel's arms.

Patchwork House Card

For this card, Bondaweb has been applied to rustic fabrics and the house components cut out and fixed in position on a piece of calico. The picture is framed with red gingham cut with fancy-edged scissors. Glue the design to corrugated card.

Patchwork Stars Card

Here, denim stars are applied to plain and chequered squares of fabric with Bondaweb. The squares are stuck to blue card and cut out with fancy-edged scissors and are then stuck to corrugated card.

Templates shown actual size

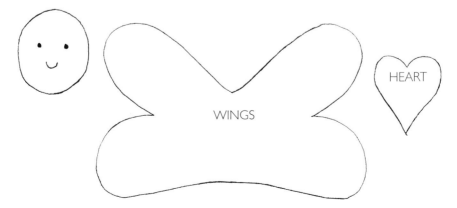

HEART

WINGS

Card Presentation

Do not lessen the impact of your beautiful hand-crafted cards by sending them in any old envelope! It is easy to make different types of envelopes, and some are described in Techniques, starting on page 17. In this chapter there are projects for more decorative card containers, including a commemorative album. Envelopes can be personalized very easily with colourful stickers and labels. Glue on some large sequins for a bit of glamour, or if the envelope is to be hand delivered, fasten it with a pretty ribbon or tassel and use sealing wax for confidentiality.

Envelopes can be created from all sorts of materials. Fabrics cut with fancy-edged scissors are very effective: address them with a fabric pen or relief paint pen. Use ready-made plastic stationery wallets and folders – they come in great colours. A sturdy corrugated plastic folder will protect a three-dimensional card enough to send it through the post if it is fastened well. If you have made an envelope from an exotic material and cannot write on it, address a luggage label and tie it on with a lucky charm attached as a little gift. Experiment with the fastenings – try gluing yarn or beaded fringing under the flap of an envelope or tie it with wire, cord or thonging.

Padded envelopes do not have to be the standard brown varieties – you can easily make your own from card or wallpaper, or you could spray-paint recycled padded envelopes to give them a new lease of life. Slip three-dimensional cards into slim boxes, either custom-made to exactly the right size or improvise with recycled packaging. Patterned paper bags can be cut open to make into envelopes.

Display favourite cards in their own handmade holders – this will not only stop them toppling over in a draught, but is also a great gift idea. You can also keep precious cards in an album or in a sealed box with the cards wrapped in acid-free tissue paper to preserve the colour and quality of the materials.

Present hand-crafted gift cards in creative
envelopes and boxes.

Decorative Envelopes

Use unusual papers and cards to make envelopes for important correspondence or to match a hand-crafted gift card. A sturdy corrugated card envelope will protect its delicate contents. Add a vibrant touch with fragments of brightly coloured papers.

YOU WILL NEED

Corrugated card
Craft knife, metal ruler and cutting mat
Bone folder (optional)
Double-sided tapes 1.2cm (½in) and
    2.5cm (1in) wide

White card
Scraps of coloured papers
Spray adhesive

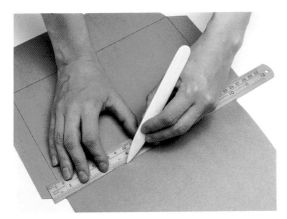

1 Refer to Making a Basic Envelope in Techniques page 17 to cut an envelope from corrugated card. Adjust the size to suit your card, and cut slanted edges for the tabs and flap. Using a bone folder or craft knife, score the envelope along the lines on the underside.

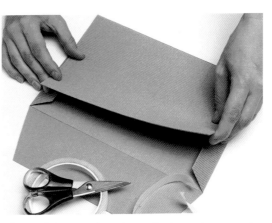

2 Fold the envelope inwards along the scored lines, then open it out flat again. Apply narrow double-sided tape to the side edges of the back. Remove the backing tape and stick the back to the front.

3 From white card, cut a label 12 x 8cm (4¾ x 3¼ in) and a border 12 x 3cm (4¾ x 1¼ in). Apply wide double-sided tape to the back of the coloured papers and cut the papers into small squares, rectangles and strips.

4 Arrange the pieces along one short edge of the label and on the border. Peel off the backing papers and stick them in position.

5 Stick the label and border to the front of the envelope with spray adhesive. Apply narrow double-sided tape to the long edge of the flap ready for fastening.

Wood-veneer envelope
A very fine veneer of real wood on a paper backing was used to make this simple envelope, which is laced with leather threaded through holes punched in the sides. The disc fastening allows the envelope to be resealed.

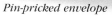

Pin-pricked envelope
This pretty wallet-style envelope is made from a rectangle of textured paper. The floral motif was pin-pricked, then the envelope folded in half and the side edges stuck with double-sided tape. The sides were then cut in zig-zags and pin-pricked. Holes punched at the top are fastened with a co-ordinating ribbon.

Mixed Media Envelopes

Do not just consider paper and card for making envelopes as there are many other materials that are also suitable. Fine foam, PVC, metal and felt all make for fun containers for your cards.

This soft, squishy envelope is made from Neoprene foam, which is a thin, pliable foam available in lots of super colours from art and craft shops. The sides are laced with plastic thonging and the envelope is personalized with the recipient's name cut in a contrasting colour and applied to the front with lots of fun Dalmatian splodges.

YOU WILL NEED

Sheet of white Neoprene foam
  30 x 20cm (12 x 8in)
Lilac plastic thonging
Scraps of Neoprene foam in pink,
  orange, red and black

Bradawl
All-purpose household glue
Double-sided tape 1.2cm ($^1/_2$ in) wide

1 Fold over one end of the sheet of white foam for 12cm (4³/₄ in) to form the envelope. The extending end will be the flap.

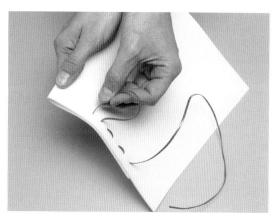

2 Hold the envelope together along one edge and pierce a row of holes approximately 1cm ($^1/_2$ in) apart and 1cm ($^1/_2$in) in from the edges of the double layers with a bradawl. Sew the lilac thonging in and out of the holes, starting on the front. Leave about 5cm (2in) extending at each end. Repeat on the other edge.

3 Make a small heart template, and cut two pink and two orange hearts from foam. Pierce a hole in the centre of the hearts and thread a heart on to the ends of the thonging. Knot the thonging on the hearts and cut off any excess.

4 Using the red foam, draw the recipient's name in the style you want, then cut out the letters. Fold under the flap of the envelope. Arrange the name on the envelope front and glue in place with all-purpose glue.

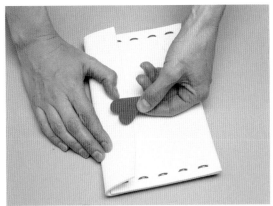

5 Cut splodges from black foam, arrange them on the envelope around the name and glue in place.

6 Place your greetings card inside the envelope. Cut a large heart from red foam. Close the flap over the envelope then stick the red heart on top with double-sided tape to seal it.

Plastic Studded Envelope

Fix a large metal eyelet to the centre of each end of a sheet of thick plastic such as polypropylene. Fold the plastic in half and fix the edges together with star-shaped studs to make a wallet envelope. Slip the greetings card into the envelope and tie a luggage label, with the recipient's name on, to the eyelets with gold ribbon.

Felt Flower Envelope

For a quick and effective wrapping for a special greetings card, fold a length of bright felt around the card and fasten it with fine ribbon. Thread flowers cut from scraps of felt on to the ribbon tails and knot the ribbon ends.

Lidded Envelopes

For these novel envelopes, a separate 'lid' is lifted to reveal the contents and can be replaced to reuse the envelope.

The grand architecture portrayed here is ideal for many occasions, maybe as a container for tickets for a special holiday or to hold a greeting commemorating a new home. The details are cut from a subtle metallic paper, or you could lightly sponge metallic paint on to thick paper.

YOU WILL NEED

Tracing paper
Thick textured white paper
Craft knife, metal ruler and cutting mat
Bone folder (optional)
Double-sided tape 1.2cm (½in) wide

Grey metallic paper
Masking tape
Spray adhesive
All-purpose household glue

1 Using the templates on page 119, trace the envelope front and lid on to tracing paper with a pencil, drawing the straight lines against a ruler. Referring to the diagram, cut the envelope from thick, textured white paper and referring to the template, cut two lids. Score along the broken lines with a bone folder or craft knife and then fold along the scored lines.

2 Apply double-sided adhesive tape along the envelope tabs. Peel off the backing tapes and stick the front over the tabs.

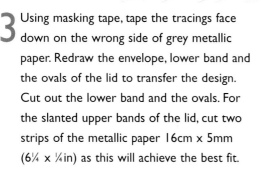

3 Using masking tape, tape the tracings face down on the wrong side of grey metallic paper. Redraw the envelope, lower band and the ovals of the lid to transfer the design. Cut out the lower band and the ovals. For the slanted upper bands of the lid, cut two strips of the metallic paper 16cm x 5mm (6¼ x ¼ in) as this will achieve the best fit.

House Envelope
Ideal for a new home, the roof lifts off this elegant house for a card or letter to be placed inside. The details are cut from co-ordinating papers and decorated with a relief paint pen.

4 Position the envelope tracing over the envelope. Spray the wrong side of the bottom band and columns with spray adhesive. Fix the pieces in place on the envelope by slipping them under the tracing so they are stuck in the correct position.

Column Token Envelope
This envelope of gold marbled paper is just the right size for presenting a gift token or money. The details are applied with a relief paint pen. Glue the back to the envelope when the paint has dried.

Enlarge templates by 200%, remembering to create a mirror image at the fold line

LID

FOLD LINE

5 Spray the wrong side of the lower and upper slanted bands of the lid with spray adhesive. Stick the lower then the upper bands in place on the lid, cutting off the ends of the upper bands with a craft knife to achieve a neat fit. Discard the cut ends. Stick the ovals to the lid with spray adhesive.

FRONT

FOLD LINE

6 Run a 5mm (¼in) wide band of all-purpose household glue along the slanted edges of the remaining lid on the wrong side, then stick the decorated lid on top. The lid slips easily over the top of the envelope.

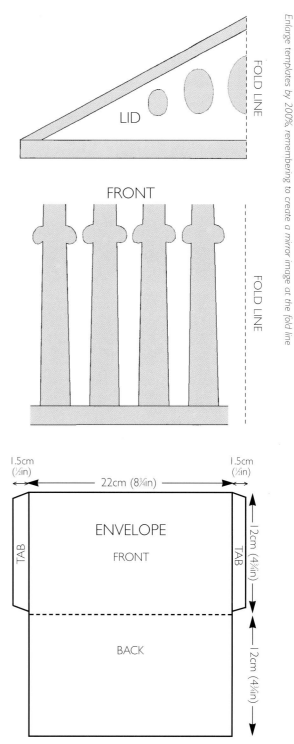

1.5cm (½in)   1.5cm (½in)

← 22cm (8¾in) →

TAB

ENVELOPE
FRONT

TAB

12cm (4¾in)

BACK

12cm (4¾in)

Commemorative Album

Make a special album to display your favourite cards in using traditional bookbinding methods. The brass posts that fasten the album are available at bookbinding suppliers and can be released to remove or add more pages. Use picture mounts to fix the cards to the pages without damaging them.

This smart album has stripes of satin ribbons applied to dupion silk. This size of album can hold two postcard-size cards on each page, or one larger card.

You Will Need

Satin ribbons – various colours between 3mm (⅛in) and 2.5cm (1in) wide
Vilene Bondaweb
Pink silk dupion fabric 30cm (⅓yd) of 90cm (36in) wide

Mounting board 3mm (⅛in) thick
Craft knife, metal ruler and cutting mat
PVA glue
Scrap of card or glue spreader
Pink paper

Thin white card
Bone folder
Hole punch
Bradawl
Pair of bookbinding brass posts

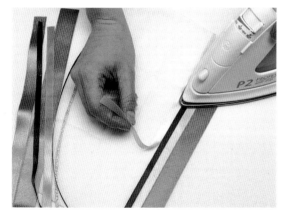

1 Cut a selection of ribbons 24.5cm (9¾in) long. Using an iron, apply the ribbons to the Bondaweb (see instructions on page 14), butting the long edges together. Carefully cut between the ribbons and peel off the backing papers.

2 Cut two rectangles of pink silk 32.5 x 24.5cm (12¾ x 9¾in) for the covers. Place the ribbons in stripes on one cover parallel with the short edges, with the first one 6cm (2½in) from the left-hand edge and the last one 2.5cm (1in) from the right-hand edge. Press the ribbons with an iron to fuse them to the silk.

3 Cut two rectangles of mounting board for the covers 24.5 x 20.5cm (9¾ x 8¼in) and two strips for the hinges 20.5 x 3cm (8¼ x 1¼in). Position the board covers on the silk covers 5.5cm (2¼in) in from the left hand edge with 2cm (¾in) on the other edges. Spread PVA sparingly on the boards and glue in place. Glue the hinge 5mm (¼in) from the cover on the left-hand side. Glue the silk over the board corners then glue the edges over the boards.

4 Cut two 27.5 x 20cm (11 x 8in) rectangles of pink paper and glue the papers centrally to the underside of the covers (and hinges) with PVA glue. Cut ten 27 x 20cm (10¾ x 8in) rectangles of thin white card for the pages. Cut ten strips of thin white card 20 x 2.5cm (8 x 1in) for the guards and then glue each guard to the left-hand edge of each of the pages. Score along the edge of the guards with a bone folder so that the pages fold easily.

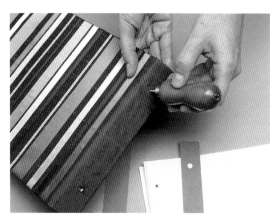

5 Using the template provided and scrap paper, cut two hole guides, cutting the page guide along the broken lines. Use the page guide as a template to punch two holes in each guard with a hole punch then use the cover guide to make two holes in each hinge with a bradawl.

6 Place the pages, guard sides up, between the covers, matching the holes. Screw the brass posts together through the holes.

Button Album

This pretty album is covered with lilac velvet and decorated with mother-of-pearl buttons stuck on in a grid formation. Chrome eyelets are fixed to the covers and beige organza ribbons used to fasten the album.

Elephant Album

Thick embossed cream paper covers this album, with a brass elephant motif sewn to a rectangle of lilac paper with a gold bead. A row of beads at each side attach the lilac paper to a larger piece of gold paper, which is then stuck to the cover. The holes on the covers are neatened with brass eyelets and fastened with a gold tasselled cord.

HOLE GUIDES

Enlarge template by 133%

Customized Card Display

Show off your gift cards in custom-made containers. Alternatively, fix them into picture frames for protection, with box frames ideal for three-dimensional cards. Cut the front off a favourite card and glue it to a piece of wood the same size, paint the edges to match the card and hang it on a wall.

A pebble fashioned from air-drying clay is very easy to make. A slit is cut in the top to slot a gift card into.

YOU WILL NEED

Air-drying clay
Kitchen knife
Strip of thick card
Acrylic paints – black and white

Ceramic tile
Artist's paintbrush
Fine artist's paintbrush
Sticky-backed felt

1 Roll a 6cm (2½in) diameter ball of air-drying clay, then roll the clay into an oval shape for the pebble.

2 Using a kitchen knife, make a cut across the top of the clay to make a slot to stand the gift card in.

3 Insert a piece of thick card in to the slot so that it does not close up whilst the clay is drying and then set the 'pebble' aside to dry completely.

4 Mix white and black acrylic paints together on a ceramic tile to make a shade of grey and paint the pebble.

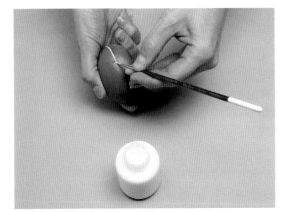

5 Use a fine artist's paintbrush to paint a stripe around the pebble with white paint. Leave to dry. Cut an oval of sticky-backed felt, peel off the backing paper and stick it under the pebble to protect delicate surfaces.

Metal Frame
Using the picture opposite as a guide, draw the frame on to tracing paper and tape it on to fine aluminium sheet. Resting on a few sheets of kitchen paper towel, press firmly with a ballpoint pen to transfer the image. Cut out the frame and the window with an old pair of scissors. From card, cut a rectangle the same size as the frame and the stand from the pop-up card on page 29. Stick the gift card to the rectangle with a glue stick, then stick the frame on top with double-sided tape. Glue the stand to the back of the frame.

Star Stand

Roll granite-effect polymer clay out flat 1.2cm (½in) thick. Stamp out a star shape using a cookie cutter. Cut a 25cm (10in) length of thick wire and coil one end into a spiral. Poke the other end upright into the centre of the star. Bake the star in the oven following the clay manufacturer's instructions.

Suppliers Index

Homecrafts Direct
PO Box 38
Leicester LE1 9BU
Tel (mail order):
   0116 251 3139
(For craft materials)

The London Graphic Centre
Tel (mail order):
   020 7240 0095
(For Artox paper products – paper, card, window mounts and envelopes)

Paperchase
213 Tottenham Court Rd
London W1P 9AF
Tel: 020 7467 6200
(For paper and card)

Paper Point
83/84 Long Acre
London WC2E
Tel: 020 7379 6850
(For paper, card and envelopes)